D0846528

Nerma and Blueberry's Staycation

by Ariana B. Farina

Illustrations by
Sunny Duran

Find more Kitty Tales in Book 1

Ariana Farina Consulting, LLC
2021

Copyright © 2021 by Ariana B. Farina

This is a work of fiction. Names, characters, places, and incidents either are the product of the author's imagination or are used fictitiously. Any resemblance to actual persons, living or dead, events, or locales is entirely coincidental.

All rights reserved. Published in the United States by Ariana Farina Consulting, LLC

No part of this book may be reproduced or used in any manner without written permission of the copyright owner except for the use of quotations in a book review. For more information, address: kittytalesthebookseries@gmail.com

Book design Sunny Duran

Editor Catherine Nichols

First paperback edition April 2021

ISBN 978-1-7360033-3-6

Contents

Dedicated to my husband Evan,
our kitties, and the rest of our family.
Thank you for all the love and support.
I love you.

Chapter 1

BRAVE KITTIES

You know Nerma is a very **fancy** kitty with black-and-white fur. But you might not know that Nerma is very brave. Most kitties hide from scary noises or new people. Not Nerma! She is **FEARLESS** like a lion.

Nerma's human sister, little Toby,
is afraid of monsters. At night, Nerma
guards Toby's bedroom door to protect
her from monsters.

Her kitty brother, Blueberry, is more
like Toby than Nerma.

Blueberry is scared of monsters. He snuggles in Toby's arms while she sleeps.

Blueberry is not very brave—or is he?

One afternoon, Nerma and Blueberry were curled up on the couch.

Their human mom walked over to them. "Dad, Toby, and I are going on a vacation to the sea. We will be back in two weeks."

Blueberry looked at Nerma. He was confused. "Vacation? Weeks? What are they?"

Nerma shrugged. They were new words to her too.

The kitties watched their human
family prepare for their so-called
"vacation." Mom and Dad pulled out
big bags with handles from a closet.
They called these bags "suitcases."

They put clothes, sandals, a floppy hat, and other items inside.

Nerma and Blueberry tried to help by watching. Kitties love to watch humans doing things. The kitties sat on top of the packed clothes in the suitcases. This was the best way to watch.

Mom bent over the kitties. "Please move somewhere else. You are in the way."

Nerma looked at Blueberry. "This is the best place to watch. I'm not moving."

She stayed put.

Blueberry did as he was told. He moved to the floor.

"Good boy!" said Mom, frowning at Nerma.

Nerma grinned back at Mom.

This made Mom laugh a little bit. Mom gently lifted Nerma out of the suitcase.

Blueberry scratched behind his ear with his paw. Even though Blueberry has extra toes on his paws, he could not reach the itch very well.

"Do you still have that itch, Blueberry? Maybe it is dry skin. Drink some water," said Mom.

He scratched his ear again and drank some water from his bowl. His ear still itched. It had itched for one whole week. It made Blueberry feel kind of **SQUIRMY.**

After the suitcases were packed, the doorbell rang. **DiNg doNg !**

"That must be Janice," said Dad.

Blueberry trembled and shook. *Oh no! Scary noises and new people!* He quickly hid in the closet.

"Nerma and Blueberry, this is Janice," said Mom.

Blueberry peered out of the closet. He saw Nerma bravely walk up to Janice and sniff Janice's foot. Nerma loves **stinky** feet smell.

"Smells a little **stinky**. She seems okay." She had to meow it loud for Blueberry to hear.

Blueberry was still shaking in the closet.

Toby called out, "Blueberry!

BLUUUUEBERRRY!

We are leaving." She walked over to the closet and slid open the door.

This made Blueberry even more scared. He did not want Janice to see him. He quickly turned around to hide his eyes.

Toby only saw Blueberry's furry behind. "Blueberry, you look scared. I will leave my doll Darla with you."

Toby set Darla down next to Blueberry. "Don't worry so much," she said. "Nerma and Darla will protect you while we are gone. Nerma is very brave."

Blueberry did not move. But he was happy to have Darla.

Toby closed the closet door. She left it open a crack. That way Blueberry could get out when he was ready.

"Bye, Blueberry and Nerma," said Mom and Dad.

Then they left with Toby for their vacation.

"Bye, kitties! See you soon," said Janice.

Then Janice left too.

After a while, Nerma went into the closet.

"Thank you for checking on me," said Blueberry. "Is Janice gone?"

"Yes, she is gone," said Nerma.

"Phew…" said Blueberry. He slowly came out of the closet.

Nerma turned to Blueberry. "Janice seemed nice."

But Blueberry was not so sure…

That evening, Nerma said to Blueberry, "Hmm, I wonder when Mom, Dad, and Toby will come home?"

Blueberry shrugged. He hoped they would come home soon because he missed them. He missed Dad stroking his fur. He missed Mom's snuggles. And he missed sleeping in Toby's arms.

Nerma missed them too.

It got later and later. Their human family did not return. Finally, the kitties laid down near the apartment front door. They fell asleep waiting for their family to come home.

In the morning, the kitties heard a key in the door.

Janice entered the apartment. "Good morning, my darling kitties."

Oh no! It was not Mom, Dad, or Toby. Blueberry quickly hid in the closet again. He cuddled Darla to feel safe and peered out at Janice.

Nerma greeted Janice right away.
Janice put out food. She also
cleaned the litter box.

After Janice left, Blueberry came out.

Night after night, the kitties slept near the front door. They were still waiting for their human family to come home.

Blueberry gave Nerma a worried look. "I wonder if our family will ever return."

One morning when Janice arrived, Blueberry hid in the closet as usual.

But this time Janice did something different. She pulled a small plastic bag from her purse.

"Kitty treats, anyone?" Janice said with a smile. She shook the bag. The treats inside the bag made a **CH CH CH** noise.

Blueberry's ears perked up when he heard the noise. He carefully poked his head out of the closet.

Janice shook the bag of treats again. "Mmm, chicken-flavored treats. Are there any kitties here who like treats?" said Janice.

"Me! Me! Me! Me! Me!" Nerma pawed at Janice's legs.

It sounded more like "Meow! Meow! Meow! Meow! Meow!" to Janice.

Janice gave Nerma some treats. "I guess ONLY Nerma likes treats."

This was too much for Blueberry to handle. He stared at the floor and tried to forget about the treats. This did not work. He walked in circles to take his mind off the treats. Walking did not help either. Even though he really loved treats, Blueberry was scared of Janice.

Blueberry turned to Darla. "Darla, can you go get me a treat?"

Darla is a doll. So Darla did not move.

"Okay, fine, you are no help. I will just run out and eat treats. Then I will run back to the closet," he told Darla. Blueberry took a big breath and ran out.

Janice gave Blueberry three treats.

He began to eat the treats. Then he heard: **Thud!** The noise sounded scary. Blueberry paused mid-crunch. *What was that?* he wondered.

Blueberry wanted to run back to the closet. But the door was closed! The thud he had heard was Janice shutting the closet door! *Oh no!*

He looked around for things to hide behind. All he saw was a skinny lamp. He ran and stood behind it.

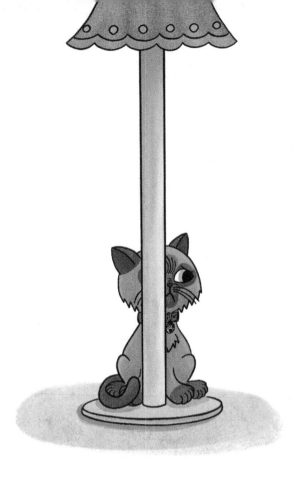

It only covered one of Blueberry's
eyes. *Oh no! Oh no!*

Something very scary was about to
happen. He was sure of it...

But nothing scary happened.

Janice gave Nerma more treats. Nerma looked very brave. She was enjoying lots of treats.

Blueberry wanted more treats too! He did not want to be a scaredy cat.

"Come here, Blueberry," said Janice. "I heard your ear itches. I can help with that."

I have been quite itchy behind my ear. Blueberry took a big brave breath and carefully walked over to Janice.

Janice slowly bent down to Blueberry and began scratching behind his ears. And guess what? The scratching really helped! Blueberry sighed with relief.

After that, Blueberry greeted Janice every day. Sometimes she played with the kitties. Sometimes she gave them treats. But their favorite were her ear scratches!

Then one day the front door opened. Janice entered. She was followed by the kitties' human family! The kitties were so happy to see them.

Mom patted the kitties on their heads. "Say goodbye and thank you to Janice."

Blueberry and Nerma purred. This was their special way of saying thanks. Janice looked very happy to hear their purrs. She waved goodbye, smiling.

Toby opened her suitcase. She took out a soft cat toy. It was a red crab.

"Look, Blueberry, I got this for you on our vacation," said Toby. "His name is Chris the Crab. Now you have your very own toy friend. Chris will help you to not be afraid."

Blueberry loved his gift. But he did not need a toy anymore. He was a brave kitty now!

Blueberry picked up Chris in his mouth. He carried him over to meet Darla and Nerma. The four friends spent the afternoon snuggling. But this time they were not in the closet.

Chapter 2

NERMA AND THE WATER MYSTERY

You know Nerma is a brave kitty. But what you might not have guessed is that Nerma is great at solving mysteries.

Nerma often watches the water coming out of faucets. Kitties have always wondered about faucet water. They want to know what happens to water after it goes down the drain.

Many kitties have tried to guess where the water goes.

Some think it comes back out of the faucet again.

Some think it goes into the fishbowl.

Others think the water vanishes like magic into the air.

But kitties never knew for sure. That is, until the day Nerma figured it out. She solved one of the great kitty mysteries of all time!

Dad was cleaning Toby's dirty plate in the sink. Nerma was sitting on the kitchen counter. The faucet water went down the drain, and Nerma watched.

Toby hates turnips. She never eats them. So one big piece of turnip was left on her dirty plate.

turnip

By mistake Dad dropped the turnip slice down the drain. **"WHOOPS!"**

Water began to fill up the sink, and Nerma jumped back, surprised.

"The turnip has clogged the drain!" said Dad.

Mom walked into the kitchen. She looked at the sink. "I can fix this by taking apart the sink drainpipe."

Mom opened up the cabinet below the sink. A pipe was underneath the sink. Mom put a bucket below the pipe. She used a wrench to remove the pipe.

All of the water from the sink fell into the bucket. **KERSPLOOSH!** The turnip fell into the bucket too.

Nerma climbed into the cabinet to get a closer look.

The water went down the pipe with the turnip! The water did not come back through the faucet. It did not go into a fishbowl or vanish! So the question was: Where did the water go after the pipe?

Hmm, what is next... It looks like the water goes down below the apartment.

Nerma remembered once when she was looking out the kitchen window. She saw holes in the ground next to the street. She had heard water rushing below those holes.

Could it be? Did the water go down
there into the ground?

Nerma knew what she must do! She had to go outside to see for herself. But how would she do that? Her family did not let her go outside.

Nerma explained her idea to Blueberry.

"No problem at all," said Blueberry. "We will get you outside with teamwork!"

Blueberry tip-toed over to Mom's purse in the living room. He carefully removed the car keys with his teeth.

Mom was sitting on the couch reading. She did not notice Blueberry. So Blueberry shook the keys in his mouth. The keys made a *jingle jingle* sound.

The noise made Mom look up. Mom, looking confused, raised one eyebrow. She stood up and walked towards Blueberry to get the keys.

The living room window was open.

Blueberry ran to it.

Mom shook her finger at Blueberry.

"Don't you dare!"

Blueberry smiled. Then he dropped the keys out the window.

Mom frowned at Blueberry. "Now I have to go get them."

Blueberry looked at Nerma. "Go stand near the front door."

Nerma ran to the front door.

When Mom opened up the front door, Blueberry scratched his claws on Mom's favorite chair.

"Blueberry! Naughty kitty!" said Mom. She ran over to stop him.

Blueberry looked at Nerma, **"NOW!"**
Nerma took her chance. She ran out
the door while Mom was not looking.

Nerma made her way to the holes on the street. It was a storm drain.

No turning back now! She wedged herself inside the storm drain. This caused her tongue to stick out and made her look quite silly.

Down she fell! She closed her eyes
to prepare to hit the bottom.
KERPLOP!

"Phew! I am not hurt," said Nerma, opening her eyes. She looked around and saw a stream of water and…a cockroach!

The cockroach was looking back at her wide-eyed.

"Hi, I'm Nerma. Where am I?"

"This is the sewer," said the cockroach.

"I want to find out where the water from the drain goes. It has led me here," said Nerma. "Do you know where all this water goes?"

"I'm Rudy," said the cockroach. "I'm new here. I used to live in a restaurant, so I don't know. But my sister Trudy might know."

Rudy turned to a wall. "Hey, Trudy!" he shouted. "This furry lady wants to know where this water goes."

Another cockroach came out from a
crack in the wall. It was Trudy.

"I will show you," said Trudy.
"But, first, I have one rule. You cannot
eat or bite me!"

Nerma agreed and nodded.

They all went further into the sewer, following the water stream. Trudy and Rudy led the way. Nerma followed close behind.

It seemed like they were walking forever. Finally, they stopped by a large pipe. Nerma saw the water going down the pipe.

"Now what?" said Nerma.

"Now you slide down the pipe," said Trudy. "All of your questions will be answered down there."

"But it is **wet**," said Nerma. "I *hate* **wet**!"

"You don't have to go. But if you want to know, you must slide down there," said Trudy.

Nerma thought for a minute. "Okay, I'm a brave kitty. I will do it."

She took a big breath and held it. Then she jumped into the pipe.

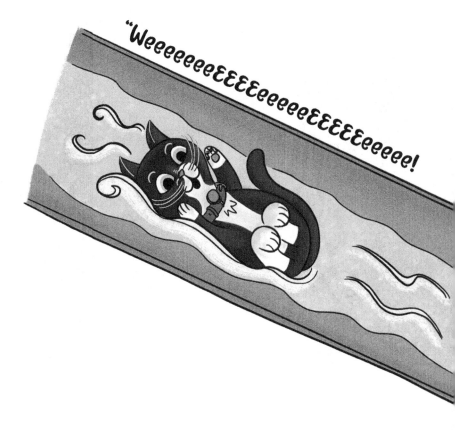

This is fun!"

It was like a waterslide! Down the pipe Nerma slid.

Then she saw a light at the end of the pipe. **KERSPLOOSH!** She fell into a big pool of water!

Nerma rose to the top of the water. *Gasp! Gasp!* She looked around. People wearing hardhats were standing near the edge of the pool. They had watched her fall into the pool. The sight of Nerma was surprising!

"Oh my! Is that a cat? What is she doing here?" said a man.

A nice woman fished Nerma out of the pool with a net.

"I can't believe you made it all the way here!" said the woman.

Me either, thought Nerma.

As the woman dried Nerma off with a towel, Nerma noticed a sign on the wall.

The woman read it to her, "Water Treatment Plant."

"What does that mean? What happens to all this water?" said Nerma.

Uh oh, what if the woman did not understand her?

But what luck! The woman understood kitty language.

"This is where we clean the water," said the woman. "Then the clean water is piped back to your faucet."

"Eureka! So the water does return again to the faucet. It just doesn't happen right away. It must be cleaned first. That makes sense," said Nerma. The great mystery was solved!

Nerma thanked the woman for her help.

"Where did you come from anyway?" said the woman.

"Check my collar," said Nerma.

The woman read Nerma's address on her collar. She offered to drive Nerma home.

Nerma shook her head. "Thank you! But I can't accept rides from strangers."

"I understand. How about we call your mom to pick you up?" said the woman.

Nerma agreed, and the woman called her mom.

When Mom came to pick her up, she was shocked to find Nerma so far from home. The two of them thanked the woman for her kind help.

Then Mom carried Nerma to the car and drove home.

Dad, Toby, and Blueberry were happy to see Nerma.

"We were so worried about you!" said Mom.

Nerma rubbed her cheek on Mom's foot. This was her way of saying sorry. Her family accepted her apology.

"So what happened? You must tell me all about your adventure!" said Blueberry.

Nerma explained everything to Blueberry.

He was truly amazed. "You are so smart!" said Blueberry.

Nerma smiled at Blueberry. She did not have to wonder about the water in the faucet anymore. The mystery was solved.

"You must let other cats know about the water!" said Blueberry.

And Nerma did just that.Kitties
came in crowds to hear Nerma talk
about the water in the faucet.

She truly earned her new nickname—
Nerma the Great Mystery Solver!

85

Chapter 3

BLUEBERRY THE BAKER

You know that Blueberry has extra toes on his paws. What you might not know is that Blueberry is a wonderful baker. But Blueberry didn't know this at first. What Blueberry did know is that he loves napping.

It was afternoon, and it was almost naptime for Blueberry. He found a nice cushion to lay down on.

Blueberry used his paws to push down on the cushion. Kitties love to knead napping spots. It makes the spot more **COMFY.**

Nerma loves Blueberry's kneading. Before she naps, she always asks Blueberry to knead her space.

"Hey, Blueberry! I'm kind of sleepy," said Nerma.

"I will take care of it!" said Blueberry.

He perfectly kneaded the chair cushion for Nerma.

"Thanks, Blueberry! You are great at kneading," said Nerma.

"It helps to purr while you do it," said Blueberry.

"Really? Why is that?" said Nerma.

Blueberry was not sure why purring made the cushion feel better. He just knew he liked to purr.

Blueberry smiled. "Um, um, ummmmmm… It just does."

Nerma nodded and chuckled.

Blueberry thought kneading was only useful for napping. Until one day…

Toby and Dad were baking. Dad turned to the kitties. "Toby and I are making my famous blueberry bread."

Blueberry was confused. Was Dad talking about him?

Blueberry looked at Nerma. "I am already standing right here. How can he make more of me?"

Nerma laughed. "Yeah, Dad is being silly."

The kitties watched Dad pull stuff out of the cabinets and refrigerator: eggs, flour, sugar, and other items. Dad put them in a big bowl. He mixed them all together.

Blueberry was surprised to see him do this.

"I thought that bowl was for me," Blueberry said to Nerma. "I sit in it when Mom and Dad are not home."

"It looks like Dad uses it for something else," said Nerma.

"Now for the finishing touch!" said Dad.

The kitties watched Dad pour a basket of round blue objects into the bowl.

Dad handed one of the blue objects to Blueberry. "Here you go, a blueberry for my Blueberry kitty."

The kitties stared at it.

Blueberry looked at Nerma. He was confused. "What is that?"

Nerma shrugged. "I don't know. A ball?"

Blueberry batted it with his paw. It didn't roll very well.

Blueberry sniffed it. Then he took a little lick. He scrunched up his face. **"YUCK!** It can't be food. It tastes bad."

"Toby, help me knead the blueberries into the dough," said Dad. He showed her how to do it.

Toby tried, but she was not very good at kneading. She just squished the dough between her little fingers.

Dad turned his back to Toby to clean up the kitchen.

Blueberry looked at Nerma. "Poor Toby. She is trying really hard. I think she might be doing it wrong."

Nerma agreed and nodded.

"I think I can help," said Blueberry. "It is like kneading before a nap."

Blueberry put his two front paws in the dough. He began purring and kneading it.

"Hahaha, Blueberry is kneading the dough!" said Toby, giggling.

Dad quickly turned around to see what Blueberry was doing.

"**NO!**" said Dad.

Blueberry looked up at Dad with surprised eyes.

Toby pointed to the dough. "Dad, look. He is pretty good at it."

Dad took a closer look at Blueberry's large feet. "Wow! It looks like you are right. His extra toes are helping knead the dough. Okay, you can keep kneading, Blueberry."

When Blueberry had finished
kneading, Dad put the dough in a pan
and the pan in the oven. After a while,
Dad took the pan out of the oven.

Mom walked into the kitchen.
"Mmm, the bread smells great."

Toby, Mom, and Dad enjoyed
eating the bread together.

Mom turned to Dad and Toby.
"This is the best blueberry bread you
two have ever made!"

"Yes, YUM! It is the best…thanks to Blueberry," said Toby.

"What?" said Mom. She was very confused.

Dad and Toby smiled at each other.

From then on, Dad always asked Blueberry for help making the bread.

And Blueberry was always happy to help. He even made up his own recipe for bread. Blueberries taste yucky to kitties. So he put fish in the bread instead.

Nerma loves to eat it! "Mmm mmmm mmmm. Soooo good!" said Nerma.

And the fish bread did taste good.
Well, to kitties the fish bread tastes
good. It might not taste as good to
humans…

the Author's Tale

Ariana B. Farina has always loved cats. As a child, after a long day at school she loved to read funny and whimsical stories about animals. As an adult, she decided to combine these interests to write books for both children and parents to enjoy. Kitty Tales: The Book Series is inspired by her own two pet cats. You can enjoy photos of her real-life adorable kitties on Instagram @ kitty_tales_the_book_series.

Made in the USA
Monee, IL
12 July 2021

73464829R00066